W9-ATL-203

FANTASTIC FOSSILS

CONTENTS

make believe ideas

WHAT ARE FOSSILS?

Fossils are the remains or impressions of ancient plants and animals. They have been **preserved** in natural materials such as stone. Fossils include huge dinosaur bones, **imprints** of leaves, the shells of sea creatures, and even footprints. Fossils give us clues to life on Earth long ago.

Velociraptor

Body fossils form from the remains of animals and plants. They include bones, teeth, and shells.

Some of the oldest animal fossils are of ancient sea creatures called trilobites. One trilobite fossil was found to date back nearly 530 million years!

Trace fossils form from materials related to living things, not from the creatures themselves. They include footprints, nests, and the **imprints** of scales and leaves.

Many fossils come from animals that are now **extinct**. Fossils tell us about these ancient creatures.

ammonite

woolly mammoth

3

FINDING FOSSILS

A **paleontologist** is a person who studies fossils. **Paleontologists** dig fossils from rocks. However, they aren't the only people to find fossils. Farmers, construction workers, and even tourists walking along beaches have made important fossil finds.

LITTLE GIRL, BIG FIND

Ancient footprints are often so big and weathered that they can be easy to miss, but in 2020, a four-year-old girl found a dinosaur footprint on a beach in Wales, in the UK. The fossil is now in a museum for people to enjoy.

brush

rock hammer

chisel

TOOLS OF THE TRADE

Paleontologists search for fossils in rocks that have been around for millions of years. They use tools such as chisels, hammers, and brushes to carefully uncover and remove the delicate fossils. Sometimes scientists use scanners to look inside fossils and rocks.

FOSSIL FARMER

In 2010, farmer John De Groot came across a fossilized jawbone when he was hiking along the Bow River in Alberta, Canada. This turned out to be the discovery of an unknown dinosaur. Scientists named it *Thanatotheristes degrootorum* after John De Groot.

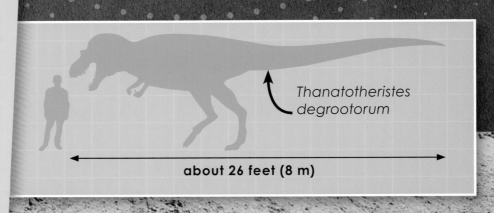

Thanatotheristes degrootorum

about 26 feet (8 m)

FAMOUS FOSSILS:
SUE THE T. REX

One of the largest and most complete *Tyrannosaurus rex* skeletons found so far is Sue the *T. rex*. Sue is named after explorer Sue Hendrickson, who discovered the fossil in 1990. Sue the skeleton now lives at the Field Museum in Chicago.

Sue lived during the Cretaceous Period, about 67 million years ago. Scientists believe the dinosaur was about 28 years old when it died. They don't know if it was male or female.

T. rex adult with its young

The skeleton is 40 feet (12 m) long. That's longer than a bus! It took 6 people 17 days to carefully remove the bones from the rock where it was discovered.

Sue the
T. rex

Because the fossil is so complete, scientists use it to learn more about the dinosaur, such as how it moved, how much it weighed, and what it ate.

HOW ARE FOSSILS FORMED?

Fossils usually form in **sedimentary rock**. This type of rock is made up of many layers of silt, stones, and sand. Once formed, fossils can last for millions of years.

Sedimentary rocks form when silt, sand, and small bits of rock are pressed into stone by the weight of the layers above.

1 A living creature dies and is buried under sand or mud, often at the bottom of the sea. The creature's soft parts, such as the flesh, rot away.

2 The sand and mud around the bones turn to rock. Deposits of minerals from the groundwater replace the bones and other hard parts of the creature, turning them to stone, too.

Igneous rocks form when lava or magma from volcanoes cools and hardens. Fossils do not form in these rocks because they would melt.

Hard **metamorphic rocks** form from extreme heat and pressure deep underground. They do not contain fossils.

3 Over time, more and more layers of rock, sand, shells, and other materials build up over the fossil.

4 As the land changes, the rock with the fossil inside may come to the surface. We find it when weather erodes the rock or we dig it up.

PERFECTLY PRESERVED

fossilized scorpion in **amber**

Not all fossils form in rock. Some living things have been **preserved** in tar, **amber**, and ice. These materials provide a great deal of information about the creatures inside.

fossilized frog

AMBER

Some ancient creatures became stuck in **resin**. When the **resin** hardened, it turned into the gemstone **amber** and **preserved** the creature inside. Because **resin** catches creatures in action, scientists can see what animals such as insects, birds, frogs, and lizards were doing when they died. They can even see what a lizard's scales looked like or the patterns on an insect's shell.

fossilized fungus gnat

TAR

At La Brea Tar Pits in Los Angeles, scientists have found more than a million ancient bones **preserved** in **asphalt**. During the Ice Age, 11,000 to 50,000 years ago, animals such as saber-toothed cats, coyotes, and birds became stuck in sticky **asphalt** and were fossilized. People are still finding more bones at this site.

young woolly mammoth found in ice

ICE

Frozen fossils are rare finds. They form when the temperature drops quickly, **preserving** the bodies of creatures that have recently died. The conditions must be just right for these fossils to form and stay frozen. The frozen fossils of Ice Age animals sometimes still have skin and hair.

FOSSILIZED HISTORY

Layers of **sedimentary rock** show the time line of Earth. Fossils found in different layers tell us which creatures and plants lived on Earth when and where. The rocks at the bottom are the oldest. Some go back nearly 4.5 billion years!

Crinoid fossils date back as far as the Ordovician Period. Even though crinoids look like plants, they are actually animals related to sea stars and sea urchins. They were common in ancient waters but are now quite rare.

crinoid fossil

Red Rock Canyon, California

modern, living crinoid

When water or wind washes away **sedimentary rock**, it can expose a bare cliff face. This allows us to see the different layers that make up Earth's surface.

ERA	SUBDIVISION	YEARS AGO
CENOZOIC	Holocene	
	Pleistocene	300,000
	Pliocene	
	Miocene	
	Oligocene	
	Eocene	
	Paleocene	66 MILLION
MESOZOIC	Cretaceous	
	Jurassic	
	Triassic	200 MILLION 230 MILLION
PALEOZOIC	Permian	
	Carboniferous	
	Devonian	400 MILLION
	Silurian	
	Ordovician	
	Cambrian	540 MILLION
PROTEROZOIC	Neo-proterozoic	700 MILLION
	Meso-proterozoic	
	Paleo-proterozoic	2.5 BILLION
ARCHEAN	Neo-archean	
	Meso-archean	
	Paleo-archean	3.5 BILLION
	Eo-archean	
HADEAN		4.5 BILLION

The first modern humans appeared.

Dinosaurs disappeared. Many more types of mammals and plants appeared.

Mammals appeared on Earth.

Dinosaurs began to rule the land.

The first land animals with a backbone appeared.

Many fossils of bacteria and fish with skeletons date back to this time.

The first known animals appeared on Earth.

Some of the oldest fossils are of tiny microorganisms, such as bacteria.

Earth was formed. It was so hot that there were no living things.

REPTILE EVOLUTION

Reptiles are cold-blooded animals that have scaly skin and lay eggs. Fossil discoveries show us how **reptiles** have changed over time—and how some haven't changed much at all.

pterosaur fossil

SEA AND SKY

Fossils show us that other giant creatures lived alongside the dinosaurs. **Pterosaurs** were winged **reptiles** that could fly, and **plesiosaurs** were large swimming **reptiles**. These types of **reptiles** are now **extinct**.

TURTLES

Turtles first appeared about 230 million years ago. Like turtles today, they had shells, laid eggs, and many swam in the ocean. Unlike turtles today, these prehistoric ancestors could reach 13 feet (4 m) long—that's about as long as a small car.

ALLIGATORS

Ancient alligator fossils look similar to the alligators alive today. That's why people sometimes call alligators living fossils.

SNAKES

Some snake fossils date from 143 million years ago. They show us that snakes used to have legs, and that the legs became smaller and smaller over time, until they eventually disappeared.

FAMOUS FOSSIL HUNTER: MARY ANNING

Mary Anning was a famous fossil hunter from the south coast of England. She was born to a poor family in 1799. Mary spent many hours searching the beach for interesting things to sell. She found lots of small fossils, as well as some of the first examples of ancient **ichthyosaur** and **plesiosaur** bones.

WHAT IS IT?

When Mary Anning dug up a complete **plesiosaur** skeleton, people thought it was a fake. With its long neck and flippers, it looked very strange. Scientists eventually agreed that it was a real fossil of an ancient swimming **reptile**.

COAST OF CURIOSITIES

Along with her big discoveries, Mary found many small fossils, such as **ammonites**. The coast where she lived is so rich in ancient fossils that it is now known as the Jurassic Coast. Thousands of people visit it every year, hoping to make their own fossil finds.

ANCIENT SWIMMERS

When she was just 12 years old, Mary and her brother found a fossilized skull buried at the beach. Mary chipped away the surrounding rock and uncovered an **ichthyosaur** skeleton. It was a swimming **reptile** that had lived almost 200 million years ago.

DINOSAUR DISCOVERIES

Dinosaurs were **reptiles** that lived during the Mesozoic Era. We have found their fossils on every continent. They include huge and tiny creatures, meat eaters, and plant eaters.

BIG BONES

The most common dinosaur finds are fossilized bones. Scientists piece them together like a jigsaw puzzle. They can then figure out what a dinosaur looked like, how big it was, how it moved, and how it behaved.

DID YOU KNOW?

Through fossils, scientists have discovered more than 1,000 different types of dinosaur— and more species are being discovered all the time.

TERRIFYING TEETH

Many different dinosaur teeth have survived as fossils. Some are as big as bananas. This sharp *Spinosaurus* tooth tells us that this type of dinosaur ate meat, such as fish. It used its pointy teeth to rip up its **prey**.

Allosaurus fossil

One leg bone can help scientists estimate the size of a whole dinosaur.

REVEALING EGGS

In the 1920s, scientists found complete egg fossils and confirmed that young dinosaurs hatched from eggs. Since then, other scientists have discovered dinosaur eggs clustered in nests. In some cases, the female dinosaur might have sat in a space in the middle of the nest to avoid crushing her eggs.

UNDERWATER WONDERS

Life on Earth began in the oceans. Simple creatures lived in the water nearly 4 billion years ago. Over time, they evolved to become more complex—and some even moved onto land. What were early sea creatures like? Fossils give us many clues.

FISHY FINDS

The first fish appeared nearly 500 million years ago. They were called jawless fish because they didn't have a bottom jaw—although some had lots of teeth. The modern lamprey is a relative of jawless fish from the past.

modern lamprey

Lobe-finned fish had short limbs with fins at the end. These limbs slowly evolved into legs for crawling on land.

SEASHELLS

Shell fossils are common because they were often **preserved** in mud and sand on the ocean floor. They once had soft bodies inside their shells. While the bodies rotted away, the hard shells stayed intact.

living coral

Armored fish had hard heads to protect them from **predators**. They are now **extinct**, and we only know about them from fossils.

COLORFUL CORAL

Corals are tiny animals with hard skeletons that join together to form colonies. These skeletons fossilize, informing us about ancient coral species.

polished coral fossil

PLANTS OF THE PAST

About 440 million years ago, plants began to invade the land. They provided food for animals, so animals began to move onto land as well. In the beginning, there weren't as many different types of plants as today. The plants that were around had adapted to survive on dry land, rather than in water—and many of their relatives still exist.

FRUITS AND SEEDS

All fruits have seeds inside. Both hard seeds and the fruit around them have fossilized. You can still see the seeds in this small fruit fossil.

FERNS

Imprints of fern fronds show that these plants date back nearly 400 million years—long before dinosaurs roamed the land. Similar ferns are still found on Earth today.

GROWTH RINGS

Tree trunks grow one new ring each year. They grow wider rings in better conditions. Fossilized trees still have visible rings. The width of the rings gives clues about how the tree grew and what the weather was like back then.

fossilized tree trunk

pine cone fossil cut in half

CONES

The seeds of trees such as pines and monkey puzzles grow inside cones. Some fossilized cones still contain seeds.

WHEN THE FIRST PLANTS APPEARED

440 million years ago
liverworts

420 million years ago
mosses

400 million years ago
ferns

310 million years ago
trees with cones

125 million years ago
plants with flowers

TRACES LEFT BEHIND

When a living thing dies, a trace of it might be left behind. Footprints, trails, burrows, and **imprints** of the plant or animal might fossilize, providing clues to what was there before.

FOOTPRINTS AND TRACKS

As ancient creatures walked through mud, they often left tracks behind them. If the conditions were right, the sun dried out the **imprints** and they turned to stone. A set of fossilized prints tells scientists about the size of an animal and how it moved.

DID YOU KNOW?

Some footprints look smaller than the foot itself would have been. For example, a *T. rex*'s print would be smaller than its foot because *T. rex* walked on its toes.

ANCIENT PATTERNS

Imprints left in the ground show the patterns of ancient shells or prehistoric leaves.

TINY TRAILS

It wasn't just the mighty dinosaurs that left their mark on Earth. Sea creatures such as worms left grooves in the rocks through which they tunneled.

SCALY SKIN

Fossilized **imprints** of dinosaur skin show us that these creatures had scales. This model shows how their skin might have looked.

TRACKWAYS

Trackways are trails of more than one footprint. By looking at how far apart each print is, scientists can work out how fast the animal was moving.

25

FAMOUS FOSSILS: MEGALOSAURUS AND IGUANODON

One of the first recorded discoveries of a dinosaur fossil was in 1676. People thought the bones might be from a giant human. It wasn't until 1824 that **paleontologist** William Buckland named the creature *Megalosaurus*. This name means "great lizard."

Megalosaurus footprint

Megalosaurus was a meat-eating dinosaur that lived 155–177 million years ago.

Iguanodon was a plant-eating dinosaur. Its teeth were the first of its fossil clues to be found.

More giant fossils were discovered in the early 1800s, with scientists agreeing that they came not from lizards but from an **extinct** animal group. In 1842, **paleontologist** Richard Owen finally declared that *Megalosaurus* and the new discovery, *Iguanodon*, were dinosaurs.

Iguanodon skull

27

TOUGH TEETH

Teeth are common fossil finds. They are a hard, tough part of the body, so they fossilize and **preserve** well. Teeth provide scientists with all sorts of stories and information about the past.

SHARKS

A shark's teeth are the hardest part of its body, so they are the most common fossils of these fierce fish. Shark teeth tell scientists how big a shark was and what it ate. Most sharks had super-sharp teeth for ripping meat.

megalodon

The biggest shark tooth found so far belonged to a prehistoric megalodon, the largest shark that ever lived. Its teeth were about three times bigger than the modern great white shark's teeth. The name megalodon means "giant tooth."

DINOSAURS

Different types of dinosaur teeth have been found. Sharp teeth belonged to meat-eating dinosaurs. Plant-eating dinosaurs had flatter teeth for cutting and grinding leaves. The longest dinosaur tooth found so far comes from a *T. rex*. It measured 12 inches (30 cm) long. That's as tall as a big soda bottle.

This skull is from a *Triceratops*, a plant-eating dinosaur.

MAMMALS

The **extinct** saber-toothed cat had two long, pointed teeth. They reached up to 11 inches (28 cm) long.

TOOTH SIZE

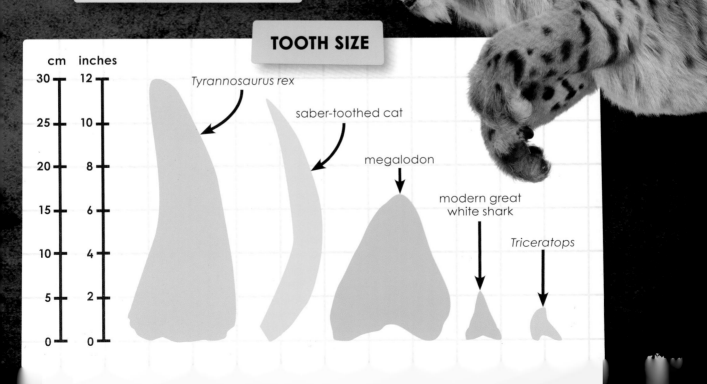

cm	inches
30	12
25	10
20	8
15	6
10	4
5	2
0	0

Tyrannosaurus rex

saber-toothed cat

megalodon

modern great white shark

Triceratops

FOSSILIZED FOOD

How do we know what the creatures of the past ate? Scientists don't just look at the shape of their teeth for hints. Sometimes they can see fossilized food in stomachs, between teeth, and in the droppings left behind.

cololite from the Miocene Period

FROM COLOLITE TO COPROLITE

Pieces of fossilized food that are still inside an animal's stomach are called **cololites**. Fossilized poops are known as **coprolites**.

cololites

coprolites

ON THE INSIDE

In 2020, scientists in Canada discovered fossilized ferns, conifer needles, and other plant material inside the belly of an armored dinosaur called *Borealopelta markmitchelli*. The **cololites** showed the exact foods this species ate.

Borealopelta fossil seen from above

IN THE TEETH

Neanderthals are **extinct** humans from the Ice Age. It was thought that they ate only meat, but scientists have discovered fossilized grains and seeds stuck in their teeth. This shows they ate a mix of both meat and plants.

TELLTALE DROPPINGS

Paleontologists examine **coprolites** to find the foods that remain inside. They provide clues to an animal's diet. **Coprolites** are not always found next to the creature that left them, so scientists must also figure out who the poop belonged to.

varied dinosaur **coprolites**

DID YOU KNOW?

The largest **coprolite** found so far belonged to a meat-eating dinosaur. It measures 26.5 inches (67.5 cm) long and is nicknamed Barnum.

FOSSIL FUELS

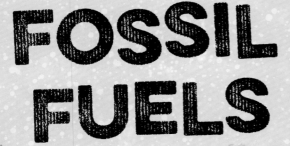

Fossil fuels are natural fuels found below the Earth's surface. They formed long ago from ancient organisms. We burn them to produce heat and light, which we can harness as energy.

Fossil fuels include coal, natural gas, and oil.

HOW FOSSIL FUELS FORM IN OCEANS

1 Many plants and animals live in the ocean. When they die, their bodies sink to the seabed.

2 Over time, thick layers of mud build up over the remains. The pressure of the weight turns the mud around the remains to stone.

Much of Texas and New Mexico was once underwater. This area is known as the Permian Basin. Today, pumping jacks dot the landscape, **extracting** oil and gas from deep wells.

EARTH FRIENDLY OR UNFRIENDLY?

Because **fossil fuels** take millions of years to develop, they are hard to replace and are known as **nonrenewable** resources. When we burn **fossil fuels**, they let off a gas called carbon dioxide, which can increase climate change.

Scientists are working to improve our use of renewable resources, such as solar and wind power. These fuels are Earth-friendly and will never run out.

3 The remains of the living things slowly turn into layers of oil and gas.

rock   gas   oil   water

4 Millions of years later, humans drill down to **extract** the oil and gas.

YOU CAN BE A SCIENTIST

Practice being a **paleontologist**. Take a look at this fossil. What can you learn about the ancient creature from the clues in its skeleton?

This skeleton belongs to the **extinct** *Dorudon atrox*: a whale that lived about 40 million years ago.

Fish bones were found inside one skeleton's stomach.

It had a long, narrow snout, useful for snapping up fish.

Its sharp teeth show that it was a meat eater.

Its short limbs were probably used as flippers for swimming. They wouldn't have supported the creature on land, so it must have lived in the water.

This *Dorudon atrox* fossil was found in the Egyptian desert.

MAKE A MODEL FOSSIL

Investigate how **trace fossils** form by making your very own model fossils at home. Follow these instructions, and then hide your fossils in sand. You can dig them up like a **paleontologist**!

- 2 cups flour
- 1 cup salt
- 1 cup warm water
- mixing bowl
- wooden spoon
- baking tray
- small toy dinosaurs, toy insects, a toy car, seashells

2 Add the warm water. Then mix and knead until you have a moist dough.

1 In a bowl, mix the flour and salt with a wooden spoon.

3 Take a small handful of the dough, and roll it into a ball. Place it on the baking tray and flatten it slightly.

4 Press your toy or shell firmly into the dough, then remove it. You could leave an **imprint** of the side of a dinosaur, a creature's feet, the pattern of a seashell, or even toy-car tire tracks.

5 Repeat steps 3 and 4 until you have used all your dough.

6 Leave the models to dry in a warm, sunny place for a few days. They are ready when they have fully hardened, just like ancient **imprints** turning to rock millions of years ago.

NOTE: Do not eat these models!

GLOSSARY

amber a yellow or brown gemstone formed from fossilized tree resin

ammonite an extinct sea creature that had a spiral-shaped shell

asphalt a thick, sticky, black liquid formed from fossilized plants and animals

body fossil a fossil formed from the remains of an animal or plant

cololite fossilized food found in the mouth, stomach, or intestines of a fossilized animal

coprolite a fossil formed from animal poop, or feces

extinct no longer found alive; died out

extract to remove something or to pull it out

fossil fuel a fuel, such as oil, coal, or natural gas, that formed from ancient plant or animal remains

ichthyosaur an extinct, ocean-dwelling reptile that looked similar to present-day dolphins

igneous rock a rock that formed when molten magma or lava cooled

imprint a mark, or shape, that forms when an object presses into a soft surface

metamorphic rock   a rock that formed under great heat and pressure underground

nonrenewable   something that cannot be replaced once it has all been used

paleontologist   a scientist who studies fossils to learn about ancient life forms

plesiosaur   an extinct, ocean-dwelling reptile with a long neck

predator   an animal that hunts and eats other animals

preserve   to stop something from rotting away or breaking up

prey   an animal that is hunted and eaten by another animal

pterosaur   an extinct flying reptile with wings

reptile   a member of a group of cold-blooded, scaly-skinned animals that crawl or creep on land

resin   a thick, sticky substance that sometimes oozes out of trees

sedimentary rock   a rock that forms when sediments are pressed together by the weight of the layers above them

trace fossil   a fossil of something connected to a living thing, such as an imprint or a nest

trackway   one or more sets of footprints forming a trail

INDEX